E.

DEALING WITH DEBT

RUTH PARSONS

Published by
Boatswain Press Ltd
Dudley House, 12 North Street
Emsworth, Hampshire PO10 7DQ

Cover design, Slatter Anderson
Illustrations by Teri Gower
Printed in Great Britain

British Library Cataloguing-in-Publication Data
A catalogue record for this book is available from the British Library
ISBN 1 873432 49 6

ESSENTIAL DEALING WITH DEBT

Contents

USEFUL TELEPHONE NUMBERS

Association of British Credit Unions	*071-582-2626*
Association of Bankrupts	*0482-658701*
Benefits Agency	*see yellow pages for your local number*
For people with disabilities	*0800-882200*
Child Poverty Action Group	*071-253-3406*
Citizens Advice Bureaux	*071-730-3469*
Consumer Credit Association of the UK	*0244-312044*
Federation of Independent Advice Centres	*051-709-7444*
LETSLink	*0985-217871*
Money Advice Centres	*0752-794631*
National Debtline	*021-359-3562*
National Federation of Credit Unions	*0274-687692*
Samaritans	*see your local telephone directory*
Shelter	*071-253-0202*

INTRODUCTION

There have always been people who want to borrow money and those willing to lend it, at a price. The credit industry makes profits by providing a service that creates both opportunity and risk. The opportunity is obtaining goods without waiting, the risk being the honouring of a credit agreement.

Credit is convenient and most people know whether they will be able to repay. Problems arise with unforeseen changes; redundancy, illness, divorce, a death or a birth. Most people now take on some debt; on average at least twice as much as ten years ago. As credit sources have increased, so have the casualties – those people whose finances have become a nightmare.

This book will help you deal with what might appear to be a hopeless situation. It will introduce you to the people who can offer expert help and advice. It will offer hope and encouragement. Face up to your problems now, and you will never have to face them again.

Normally, doing nothing means that nothing changes; but when dealing with debt, doing nothing means the situation deteriorating out of control. You have already taken your first positive step. Don't stop now.

Follow the *10 POINT PLAN* and you will soon resolve your difficulties.

TEN POINT PLAN OF ACTION

1. **ADMIT THE PROBLEM TO YOURSELF**
2. **TRY NOT TO PANIC OR FEEL GUILTY**
3. **WORK OUT YOUR PERSONAL FINANCIAL DETAILS**
4. **SEEK APPROPRIATE HELP AND ADVICE**
5. **CONTACT YOUR CREDITORS**
6. **SHOW YOUR WILLINGNESS TO SETTLE YOUR DEBT**
7. **FORMULATE A BUDGETING PLAN**
8. **CONSIDER WAYS OF INCREASING YOUR INCOME**
9. **DEVELOP ASSERTIVENESS**
10. **KEEP GOING TOWARDS THE END OF THE TUNNEL**

ADMIT THE PROBLEM TO YOURSELF

Don't bury your head. Practical **difficulties do not go away** if ignored and you will only delay the recovery. If so far you have not been facing up to your problems, take heart. Reading this means that you're already making a change for the better.

Do any of the following seem familiar?

- *Paying bills on time has become difficult*
- *Money is a constant worry*
- *I am always juggling with money*
- *My problems are getting worse and I can't cope*
- *Dealing with my finances makes me feel frightened and alone*
- *I can't see a way out.*

Most people's difficulties stem from changed circumstances; divorce and redundancy are the main reasons. This change causes strain affecting your ability to think and manage. A vicious circle begins – reduced income – reduced ability to cope – muddled and terrifying state of affairs.

Accepting that our actions and reactions have created the circumstances is hard, but it's a valuable lesson on how to avoid the same mistake again. **Managing money is a skill, and everyone makes mistakes.**

TRY NOT TO PANIC OR FEEL GUILTY

Don't react emotionally. Keep calm and accept things as they are. **Do not borrow** to pay off what you owe – unless it's a consolidation loan arranged by your debt counsellor with your bank.

Don't blame yourself or others. Admitting responsibility is sensible, adult behaviour but self-blame is destructive and undermines the energy you need to cope. **Positive action, is required.** Congratulate yourself for coping this far – then get on with what needs to be done.

WORK OUT YOUR FINANCIAL DETAILS

You must know your financial situation before you can sort it out. Set down, item by item, the money you have coming in, your regular outgoings and how much you owe. **Don't put off doing it.** This will be a major step towards sorting out the problem. First, list your income before anything has been bought or paid for. Include wages, any benefits you claim, maintenance payments and any other regular source.

Next, you need to know where the money goes. Payments like mortgage or rent, fuel bills, child-minding charges etc are easy to list as they tend to be the same each month. Food bills, clothing costs, travelling etc will vary.

If your problems are not too pressing, you can get an idea of what you spend by carrying a notebook and writing down whatever you spend and on what. Divide it into sections – food, clothes, household expenses, entertainment etc. You will soon see the average amounts being spent on each category showing you where to economise. It is a surprise to see just how much is spent on non-essentials.

Calculate what you need to cover the essentials, eg a roof over your head, essential household expenses, feeding and clothing the family. The remainder should be divided between your creditors on a pro-rata basis. This means that if one debt is a quarter of what you owe, then you offer your creditor a quarter of the available money you have left.

Work out pro-rata payments using the following example:

- Income available to pay creditors – £40
- Total balance owed each month – £100 comprising of three debts – £45, £25 & £30

- 1st debt of £45 – multiply by £40 *(available income)* = £1800
  Divide by £100 *(amount owing)* = **£18**

- 2nd debt of £25 – multiply by £40 *(available income)* = £1000
  Divide by £100 *(amount owing)* = **£10**

- 3rd debt of £30 – multiply by £40 *(available income)* = £1200
  Divide by £100 *(amount owing)* = **£12**

The **£18, £10** and **£12** are the amounts to offer to your creditors as they total your available income – **£40.** Debt counsellors use this system and can work out a fair repayment plan with you.

SEEK APPROPRIATE HELP & ADVICE

Many organisations offer impartial financial advice. They help with *Income and Expenditure* sheets, advise how to trim expenses or add to your income. They will help write to creditors; some even do this for you. Pride, embarrassment and fear force many people to shoulder the heavy burden alone. **Share your troubles** with a trained debt counsellor and keep the problem in perspective. Names of organisations able to offer help and support are listed in the A-Z section.

CONTACT YOUR CREDITORS

You must do this as soon as making repayments has become difficult. If you have put off getting in touch, **don't delay further.**

With banks and building societies, make an appointment for a personal visit as problems can be sorted out more easily face to face. With a credit card company, a phone call or letter is the next best thing. Most creditors will work out a feasible repayment plan if you contact them before they have to pursue you. They want to avoid costly legal action and so do you. Look for contact telephone numbers on your statements as some companies have helplines to discuss problems.

The response from your creditor may be more amenable than expected. Even if you receive an unfriendly reception, remember that **it is in the interests of both parties to work together.**

DISPLAY YOUR WILLINGNESS TO SETTLE YOUR COMMITMENTS

A creditor will watch for your attitude. Show that you'll try to settle the debt quickly and they are likely to be helpful. Creditors can help by extending the repayment time or even suppressing interest. These measures may be used if you show a committed approach to clearing your debt.

Seek expert help from debt counsellors at the Citizens Advice Bureau to work out a plan to repay priority and non-priority debts.

Once your creditors get a clear picture of your financial situation and see your efforts to repay they are more likely to be cooperative

FORMULATE A BUDGETING PLAN

- *Weekly income* £100
- *Weekly outgoings* £101 = *Misery*

- *Weekly income* £100
- *Weekly outgoings* £ 99 = *Happiness*

If your outgoings exceed your income, you may think budgeting is a waste of time. But having worked out your income & expenditure and negotiated payments with creditors you can make a plan and stick to it. Your debt counsellor will ensure that you keep a reasonable amount to live on.

If dealing with creditors alone, **ensure you have enough for essentials** like shelter, food, fuel, clothes and travelling to work. If you do not, your health and prospects will suffer, so too your chance of resolving matters.

Find ways to stretch your money. It is hard to alter a lifestyle, but worth it when you are finally free from the pressure of debt.

CONSIDER WAYS OF INCREASING YOUR INCOME

Could you find a better paid job, or get a rise in your present one? If not, perhaps an extra part-time job would help your income. Do you qualify for Social Security benefits? Visit their office and check. Have you unwanted items you could sell? Try a small ad in the local paper. Car-boot sales are very popular and for a fee you can sell unwanted toys, clothes and household items – although remember buyers are looking for bargains, so expect to haggle. Could a hobby or special talent be profitable? Can you cook, do practical jobs around the house and garden? Are you an expert on any subject – would anyone pay you to give tuition? Give thought to how you could use your abilities to boost your income. Your long term interests might be helped by extra qualifications to increase your promotion chances. Check what night classes are on offer locally or consider an Open University course.

DEVELOP ASSERTIVENESS

Apart from the practicalities of debt problems you should give thought to what caused them. The chances are that you are not the only one involved and affected. Maybe a partner or family member is being unreasonable or irresponsible with your joint finances. If they are unco-operative, you may feel your good intentions are being sabotaged.

Confrontation is difficult and uncomfortable, but just as it was important to face up to the situation, it is just as necessary to confront the others involved. If strict money management is not practised by everyone involved then the good work being done to discharge the debts will be wasted.

Assertiveness is often confused with aggressiveness, yet they are very different. Our behaviour falls into three broad categories – aggressive, passive and assertive.

Aggressive behaviour is overbearing, parental, commanding and manipulative.

Passive behaviour is a fear of what the other person might say or do and appears as timid, childish and ineffectual.

Assertiveness is a set of sensible, reasoned, adult actions and responses, the objective being to reach a conclusion which respects and benefits all concerned.

Perhaps by keeping quiet about how you feel *(passive)* or by shouting, arguing or complaining *(aggressive)*, it has been impossible to agree how your finances should be handled.

Use assertiveness to deal with both your joint finances and relationship. Keep calm, avoid mud-slinging, stick to the facts and describe your feelings. **Good communication is about openness, honesty and a desire for a common aim,** it is not about blame or shifting responsibility to someone else. Everyone makes mistakes. Showing compassion is a good way to get a responsible attitude from the other person.

If at first your attempts fail, do not give up. Request cooperation unemotionally but with determination. Listen to the other person and be prepared to compromise. As communication improves, so will the ability to work together.

KEEP WORKING TOWARDS THE LIGHT AT THE END OF THE TUNNEL

DON'T be downhearted if you find debt frightening. There is **always** a solution, even if it sometimes appears remote. Create a mental picture of what you want, and where you are going; of how you will be when you have cleared your debts. Don't lose sight of that or you'll lose hope. What do you want? A life where you're able to afford luxuries now and then, free from the dread of bills arriving in the post? Create an image of a successful conclusion and keep working towards it. **A positive attitude is crucial to success.** Mentally experience the satisfaction of beating your problems and enjoying life and your expectations will become a reality.

A TO Z

A

ACCOUNTANTS

A self-employed person with debt problems should consult an accountant. They will be able to advise on tax problems and provide a professional approach to creditors. Not everyone will benefit from an accountant however, and paying for their services will add to your debt. Alternatively look for advice from a debt counsellor providing a free service. *see Advice, Citizens Advice Bureaux and Legal Aid*

ADAPTING TO CHANGE

We are constantly faced with new circumstances. Mostly these are gradual and we acclimatize easily. The bigger the change the harder it can be to adjust. A change in financial circumstances is difficult to cope with and it's easy to continue in the same old way. Carrying on spending when you haven't enough money will only make the problem worse. Sit down quietly and work out the best ways of adapting. **Changes will have to be made** to attitude and behaviour if the problems are to be sorted quickly.

Think what you can do to improve matters. List the actions you could take, then work your way through to sort out the best courses of action. Sometimes an unlikely idea may prove a valuable part of the solution and every positive step you take will make some improvement.

ADDICTIONS

An addiction of any kind *(alcohol, gambling, drugs etc)* is a way of opting out of reality. Debt problems cause misery and heartache. If you resort to forms of escape rather than deal with the cause of your distress, you add to the sum total of your despair. **Facing up to problems will reduce the stressful effects** instead of prolonging them. There are excellent organisations which offer counselling and support. Talk to your GP or contact the relevant organisation directly. The Samaritans or Citizens Advice Bureau will give you details of Alcoholics Anonymous, Gamblers Anonymous and the Drug Advisory Service. You can also find their numbers in the telephone directory. **Don't suffer alone,** get help now.

ADMINISTRATION ORDERS

An Administration Order, directed by the Court or applied for by a debtor, is a way to deal with multiple debts totalling less than £5000. Instead of dealing with them separately, the Court sets the total amount of the instalments and apportions them pro rata to all the different creditors. This allows the debtor a breathing space and headway is made with clearing the debts. An advantage for the debtor making regular payments is protection from other enforcement actions *(the exceptions to this being disconnection by fuel boards and repossession by mortgage companies).*

ADVICE

Seeking **advice from an experienced debt counsellor is the most important thing** you can do. Enlisting help means that you will be guided through a difficult time. Counsellors at the Citizens Advice Bureaux are trained to deal with personal debts. They listen sympathetically and help with the problems of dealing with your creditors, often liaising to arrange for you to repay your debts. They will help you budget to ensure your income is used efficiently, while making sure you do not suffer hardship.

The following have people available to give advice on debt and who will act in your, the consumer's, interest.

- ***Citizens Advice Bureaux***
- ***Benefits Agency***
- ***Federation of Independent Advice Centres***
- ***Housing Aid Centres***
- ***Legal Advice Centres***
- ***Money Advice Centres***
- ***National Debtline***
- ***Social Work Departments***
- ***Trading Standards Departments***

Some creditors have telephone helplines *(check your statements)*. They will be primarily concerned with recovering their money, but some give generalised guidance on how to handle a debt situation.

ALCOHOL

see addictions

ANGER

Anger usually arises from a feeling of helplessness. When in debt, you are bound to feel matters are beyond your control. The anger could be directed at

yourself for getting into the situation in the first place; or aimed at someone you feel has contributed to the position in which you find yourself. *see point 9 in the 10 point plan – Develop Assertiveness*
Expressing the fact that you are angry is good, but if the anger continues it can be destructive to you, your relationships and the situation. **Harness the anger and use it to do something positive.** *see Do something*

APR

APR stands for Annual Percentage Rate and varies between creditors. Interest charges and all costs should be included when the rate is calculated, giving a standard way of comparing the cost of credit. Some companies do not include certain charges, *for example a setting-up fee for a loan,* **so always check carefully before signing any agreement.** The APR affects the amount you pay for credit – so compare rates very carefully.

ARRANGEMENTS WITH CREDITORS

Many people are afraid to approach their creditors when having problems as they think that there are only two options – make full payments or be taken to court. This is rarely the case. Creditors are realistic in their demands for payment when they are satisfied that the customer is not in a position to keep up the original agreement. Although not ideal, it is preferable to work out a repayment plan to ensure the best chance of recovering the money, even if it does takes longer than agreed and cuts down the profit. There are various ways in which the creditor can make it easier for the customer to clear the debt. Each case is dealt with individually and it is in the interests of both parties to reach agreement quickly.

ARREARS

If you fall behind with payments you are said to be in arrears. This amount of money is owed in addition to the regular payments you are making. To clear the arrears you will need to make your regular payments plus an additional sum until the account is in order.

If your problems are temporary, a creditor will most likely allow you to pay an agreed monthly sum to straighten matters, especially if you have made an honest approach about the situation. If the problem is severe tell your creditors and **seek help** from a debt counsellor to work out a repayment plan.

ASK

Always ask if you are not sure. When buying anything on credit read the agreement terms and conditions thoroughly before signing. When you have, ask about any point which is not absolutely clear. **It is especially important to read the small print of an agreement.**

Ask the retailer how much an item is going to cost before you buy *(ie stated price plus the interest)*. Ask if the interest rates are fixed for the term of the agreement or likely to change.

Ask your debt counsellor to explain any aspect of the process of debt recovery if you are unsure. The more aware you are, the more confidence you will have in dealing with your financial affairs.

ASSETS

Financial assets are money or possessions which belong to you and can be realised *(sold or used)* to repay debts.

ATTACHMENT OF EARNINGS ORDER

If you do not make payments set by a Court, the creditor can apply for an attachment of earnings order. Your employer is then ordered to deduct money from your wages and pay it directly to the Court. **It is possible to explain to the Court if this would cause a severe problem** *(such as losing your job)* but failing to comply with their final decision would incur a prison sentence.

Should circumstances change, apply again to the Court who can revise the situation.

ATTITUDES TO MONEY

Have you ever thought about your attitudes towards money and how they affect the way you manage financially? *see Children*

Is it a way of life to you to borrow on credit – 'Everyone does it?' Do you believe it brings happiness, trouble, or power? Do you believe it is best to save for a 'rainy day' or 'live now, pay later?' Do you feel you should have what other people have? Is money the root of all evil or there to enjoy? Do you wish that you had more money, that you could never have enough? Do you plan ahead or spend what you have, regardless? The way you look at money could reveal the answer to why you have problems and how to improve the situation. If you know money burns a hole in your pocket, then you should pay special attention to saving some of your income. If you believe you will never have enough, maybe you are not pushing towards achieving your potential. **Develop confidence in yourself.** Be adventurous in believing what you can achieve. Work out whether your attitudes to money are positive ones – if not, change them.

AVOIDING BANK CHARGES

Bank charges can mount quickly and become a large part of your debt. There are steps you can take to ensure charges are kept to a minimum. Keep a close watch on your balances and make transfers from one account to another to avoid going overdrawn. Arrange an auto transfer facility with your bank to do this for you. Have statements sent frequently so that you know the state of your account/s. If you are going to be overdrawn ask the bank for an agreed overdraft facility to keep charges as low as possible. An overdraft will fluctuate, the rates are linked to base rate and may alter. When you withdraw money from a service till, update your balance when you get home. Forgetting to record the transaction may mean that you go overdrawn and incur charges.

B

BAILIFFS

Ignoring a Court Summons or failing to make payments imposed by the Court will result, sooner or later, in Bailiffs calling at your home to demand payment. If you have not got the money they have legal authority take goods in lieu of your debts. *see Distress Warrant*. They have the authority to evict or remove you from your home and sell it to clear your debts. *see Repossession*

Your possessions will be sold and should the amount raised be insufficient to cover your debt, you could be made bankrupt or even sent to prison.

To avoid such action **it is vital to reply promptly** and properly to a Court Summons, to attend hearings when required to do so and make an effort to make the set payments. Seek help on how to deal with a Summons.

BANKS

If you are having money problems then your bank will want to know as soon as possible. They will have noticed that you are having a struggle and are likely to be sympathetic if you are honest about the situation. Take statements of other debts when you see them, these will be taken into account when arranging repayment schedules. Creditors prefer regular payments, even if they are reduced, to no payments at all. If the bank calls in your debt and you cannot comply, **make an appointment immediately.** If you do not make contact, you will be registered with a credit reference agency precluding you from any future credit. *see Credit Reference Agencies*

The bank will advise how to contact other creditors but will mainly be concerned with their own debt. Take your credit cards with you, as you will probably be asked to cut them up there and then.

BANKRUPTCY

A bankruptcy petition is a demand that you pay all your debts in full and can originate in two ways; it is either filed against you by a creditor or you file your own petition.

Many people filing for bankruptcy themselves, do so because they panic and feel under unbearable pressure from creditors. **In most cases experts would advise against it.** There are several options open before resorting to making yourself bankrupt. Seek expert advice – an accountant or the Citizens Advice Bureau would be able to help.

If you are forced into the position of becoming bankrupt then the control of your financial affairs is taken out of your hands. The official receiver or trustee has a legal right to dispose of your property and assets as they see fit. You cannot interfere.

Bankrupts are not allowed to hold certain public offices, can no longer handle finances, or hold company directorships. Solicitors and accountants are denied the right to practise. Bankrupts cannot obtain a mortgage and are required to inform potential creditors that they are bankrupt, so individual decisions can be made whether to allow credit.

The strain of bankruptcy is enormous and a sense of failure overwhelming. Family members are also affected greatly. It is essential to accept all the help and support on offer. Talking it through with a counsellor can give tremendous relief. *see Counselling and Samaritans*

BENEFITS

The Benefit Agency benefits can help in a wide range of financial hardship circumstances. The Benefit Agency has free leaflets explaining what is available. You can ring on *Freephone 0800 666555* write to: *Leaflets Unit • PO Box 21 • Stanmore Middlesex • HA7 1AY*
For people with disabilities use *Freephone 0800 882200*

BLACKLISTED

see Credit Reference Agencies

BORROWING

When you borrow or take on a credit agreement, ensure the company is reputable. Check the terms so that you know exactly the full amount being repaid *(with interest and charges included)*. **Check the rates with other companies to ensure you are getting the best deal.** Be certain that you will be able to find the repayments without it leaving you short or having to cut down on essentials. Finally, ask yourself whether the advantages will outweigh the disadvantages – will the amount of benefit you get, be worth the cost?

BUDGET ACCOUNTS

These accounts are designed to even out your expenses. The bank will ask you to list regular payments like gas, electricity, insurance, television licence etc. and to add an agreed amount for inflation. That total is divided by 12 and you sign a standing order to transfer between your current and budget accounts every month. As the bills arrive, you pay with a budget account cheque, whether or not there is enough money in the account to cover it. At the end of the year the money you have paid in will be approximately that of your outgoings, with the total cost being spread over the year.

BUDGETING

Successful budgeting means keeping your expenditure **within the limit of your income.**
Financial problems start when expenditure exceeds income. Budgeting under these circumstances involves drawing up a detailed and accurate account of a person's financial situation and finding ways of either increasing income or cutting expenditure. A list of essential outgoings is drawn up, including those to be dealt with first to allow the debtor a home, food, clothes, warmth and essential services. Any remaining income is divided to pay non-priority debts on a pro-rata basis *(the bigger debts being apportioned a bigger share of the available money).*
Sustained efforts to remain within a budget while still making agreed repayments will reduce your debts and bring about financial stability. *see also Economising*

BUILDING SOCIETIES

Mortgage arrears are priority debts and **must be dealt with immediately.** People feel either threatened, or complacent because they don't think they can be turned out of their house, and allow arrears to mount. Both views are extreme. Each case is assessed individually, depending on circumstances and the debtors resolve to discharge his or her debt. Go and see the manager and tell him why you are finding it difficult to make payments. Increasingly building societies use debt counsellors as they realise that to demand payment when the money is not available is fruitless, and prefer to work out a realistic repayment plan with you.

Your building society can repossess your house *see Shelter*, but this is mostly used as a last resort. Face up to your problems, keep lines of communication open, make agreed payments and it is highly unlikely that you will lose your home.

C

CALCULATORS

Use a calculator when shopping if you are on a tight budget. Tot up the items as you go round the store so that you know how much you are spending. If over-budget, return some luxury items to the shelves. Use the calculator to adjust the balance in your cheque book when you write a cheque or withdraw money. A calculator helps to make the job of budgeting and keeping financial records much easier.

CHILDREN

Our attitudes to money start in childhood. If children are taught sensible money management, they will have few problems later. It is never too early to teach them to handle money proficiently.
Allocate pocket money after working out a reasonable budget – enough to cover bus fares, lunch money etc – with an extra amount to save or use for what they want. If you give your children the responsibility of dealing with their own money and resist the temptation to make up the difference if they overspend, they will learn early how to save and spend wisely.
Paying your child for extra jobs around the home, over and above normal family chores, encourages initiative and responsibility. If older children take part-time jobs they will gain confidence and will realize that money is not available on demand. They will see that it is mostly hard-earned, so will come to respect its value. Show them the family budget, how income and expenditure need to be balanced, how expensive certain items are, as well as the cost of

services, telephone bills for example!
Encourage them to save. Banks and building societies have incentives for young savers to open accounts and whatever is bought with money earned through patience and hard work will be appreciated a lot more.

CITIZENS ADVICE BUREAUX

CAB give advice on any subject but a large percentage of enquiries are debt related. They have specialised debt counsellors available and as the amount of credit has increased their experience has become extensive.
They are listed in the telephone directory and you can usually visit without an appointment, although check first as you may need one if they are particularly busy.
Their role is to act as a responsible, independent third party, advising debtors and negotiating with creditors. Creditors know that if CAB handle the case, the situation will be fairly serious. They will also know that the debtor will be given sound advice and any offers of payment made will be realistic. The creditor will be more likely to accept reduced payments. After a repayment plan has been agreed they will require the CAB to send regular updates, so that necessary adjustments can be made if your situation changes.

COMMITMENTS

In a financial context, commitments are all your outstanding debts, ie whatever you owe on credit.

CONFIDE IN SOMEONE

Sometimes the worst part of a problem is the worry going round and round in your head. Reduce your burden by sharing it with a friend or confidant. You need someone that you can trust, who will listen sympathetically and non-judgementally and will be sparing with advice *(which is best given by an expert on the subject)*. Releasing the pressure by talking about your problems gives a sense of relief and enables you to look at life more objectively.

CONSOLIDATION LOAN

This means amalgamating all your debts into one loan with a single monthly repayment. The loan will cover all credit commitments – credit cards, bank loans, hire purchase agreements etc. Payments are spread over long periods, reducing monthly outgoings in an effective way of repaying debt.

If granted this loan, you will need settlement figures from your original commitments and the money will probably be released directly to your creditors. Provided you keep within the limits of your budget, this could be a very workable solution.

A debt counsellor can advise whether a consolidation loan would be useful in your circumstances. Apply only to reputable credit companies – Banks, Building Societies or well known credit organisations. **Never ever borrow from obscure money lenders** *see Loan Sharks* as repayment charges will be extremely high, recovery methods dubious and you will find yourself worse off than before.

CONSUMER CREDIT ASSOCIATION

The Consumer Credit Association is the trade association for businesses operating in the credit market. It takes pride in its reputation of cooperation with Government, Trading Standards Departments and organisations such as Citizens Advice Bureaux and Money Advice Centres.

Its Code of Practice ensures members conduct their business lawfully and responsibly and with integrity. Members are required to provide clients with information on credit protection insurance and must act responsibly in both marketing and advertising. The Code forms a comprehensive structure to protect the consumer. The Association monitors its members' performance, thus affording them a reputation for honest and fair trading. They welcome credit related enquiries and offer advice and guidance where possible.

The Consumer Credit Association of The United Kingdom • Queens House • Queens Road Chester CH1 3BQ Telephone: 0244 312044

CONTACT YOUR CREDITORS

When you have debt problems the most important thing to do is to contact your creditors. They may be aware of your difficulties because of late or missed payments. They will want an explanation but will be eager to sort out problems before they escalate.

It takes courage to admit your difficulties and fear stops or at least delays many people making that initial move until matters become far worse. At an early stage the problem may be relatively minor and easily dealt with.

The person reading your letter or answering your telephone call will have sympathy with your circumstances. Be polite and straightforward in your approach – coming over as aggressive or offensive will alienate the very people who can help and will only complicate your situation. Everyone finds it easier to be constructive with someone whose manner is affable and positive.

Your creditor may have a telephone helpline to deal with accounts in financial difficulty – someone well used to debt problems. Explain concisely what has caused your difficulties. Money is hard to find for many people due often to unemployment or redundancy. Divorce or illness create further demands on finances. Usually a combination of factors contributes to a debt situation and yours will probably be similar to many your creditors are presently dealing with.

COOLING OFF PERIOD

Credit agreements should contain a cooling off period allowing you an amount of time after signing the agreement to reconsider. This gives you time to decide whether you have made the right decision, away from any pressure from the salesperson. The length of time may vary so check this at the time of signing. Bear in mind that you may not have the right to cancel, or you may lose it, if you sign on the trader's business premises. A similar situation exists if a deal is arranged on the phone, even if you sign the agreement at home. If you change your mind, sign and return the form that you can either detach or that is printed on the reverse. Alternatively send a letter within the specified time.

COST

When purchasing on credit make sure that you

know the full amount to be repaid before signing the agreement. If taking out a loan, ask about additional fees *(an arrangement fee or early settlement fee)*. These can increase the original amount and you may have to repay much more than you expected.

COUNSELLING
Counselling is simply talking over your problems with someone trained to listen and give sound advice. Debt counsellors have special experience of debt problems. They are qualified to give impartial advice on the best ways to sort out problems and discharge debts whilst ensuring that individuals and their families suffer as little as possible in the process.

COUNTY COURT JUDGEMENTS
Having a Court Judgement against you will usually prevent you obtaining further credit.

CREDIT
To give credit is to trust a person's ability and intention to pay for goods or services later. Obtaining credit is a privilege that carries with it the reputation of solvency and honesty. Failure to pay financial obligations threatens that reputation, and any future borrowing capacity.

CREDITOR
A creditor is one who gives credit for money or services and to whom a debt is owing.

CREDIT CARDS
A credit card is an authorisation to obtain goods on

credit. Using credit cards can be very convenient and safer than carrying large sums of money. It enables you to tie together many transactions with single monthly payments to the credit card company and has the advantage of delaying repayment by several weeks. Provided the bill is cleared each

month charges are minimal. This service is useful for those who spend within their limits and have sufficient to cover at least a substantial monthly repayment
It is very easy to overspend with credit cards, possi-

bly because no cash changes hands and the reality of the situation is slightly blurred; especially if you do not want to think about how much you are spending. Interest rates charged by credit card companies are usually very high and by making minimum repayments your debt may well increase dramatically. Continuing to use your card in these circumstances is inviting disaster. The sensible course of action is to cut the card in two and return it to the company. When your account has been cleared, then you can always review the situation.

CREDIT REFERENCE AGENCIES

The main job of Credit reference agencies, licenced by the Office of Fair Trading, is to supply information to creditors so they can assess the risk when lending to a customer.
The creditor will apply to an agency to:
Verify the customer's identity by checking names held on the electoral register – forename, surname, postal address and length of residence. Look for any county court judgements recorded in the last six years from information compiled by the Registry Trust on bankruptcies, serious default and 'written off' debts. Provide information on the customers past and present credit record.
Information supplied is purely factual and it is up to individual creditors to make their own lending decisions. If you are refused credit, you can obtain a copy of the information held about you and have any mistakes put right. Ask which agency was used and send a written request for the information, together with the required fee.

CREDIT SCORING

This is used to assess how reliable the person applying for a new account will be, when it comes to repaying a debt. It works by using certain variables such as sex, age, employment, status, and address, together with information from credit reference agencies regarding the past credit record. When all this is put together, a decision is made by the creditor whether to accept you as a customer.

CREDIT UNIONS

Credit Unions are financial cooperatives, providing convenient savings and low cost loans. They are owned and run by their members, who have to have some sort of common bond. This could be a bond of doing the same sort of job, living in the same area, or members of the same organisation such as a particular church.

Each Credit Union encourages responsible saving and borrowing. Some offer financial advice and debt counselling.

Members are required to save either weekly or monthly for a certain period of time and are then eligible to apply for a loan.

These are mostly for domestic purposes and carry a very low rate of interest, offering the cheapest unsecured credit in the country.

Association of British Credit Unions Ltd
Unit 307 Westminster Business Square
339 Kennington Lane
London SE11 5QY *Telephone: 071 582 2626*

National Federation of Credit Unions
Credit Union House • 102 Tong Street • Bradford
West Yorkshire BD4 6HD Telephone 0274 687692

D

DANGER SIGNS

If you are having financial problems, the chances are your creditors have noticed too. Overdue payments are obvious signs. An explanation of the circumstances will help them to decide what action to take. Maybe the difficulty is temporary, in which case no further action need be taken as you will soon be able to catch up with your repayments. If your difficulties are more serious, then **organise a repayment plan as soon as possible.**

You are the best person to spot the danger signs involving your finances, well before your creditor picks up the signals. It may mean you are able to avert problems before they get serious; simply cutting back on non-essentials might make it possible to find the extra money needed to cover monthly commitments. *see Economising*

Ignoring danger signs will make matters worse.

DATA PROTECTION

The Data Protection Act of 1984 applies to all information stored on computers and which relates to living individuals. It does not cover information processed manually or held in ordinary paper files, or information relating only to a company. The Act requires the users of such information to apply for permission to collect it and to do so in a fair and lawful manner. It gives the individual whose information is recorded the right of access to it and to have it corrected or deleted. Anyone who has personal data held about them is entitled to a copy. Write to the company concerned with your request

– there may be a charge. If the data is inaccurate you can complain or apply to the Courts for correction or deletion of it. If damage has been caused you can seek compensation.

DEBT
Amount of money, goods or services owing.

DEBTOR OR DEFENDER
Someone who owes money, a service or duty.

DEFERRED PAYMENTS
Paying for goods or services, usually by instalments, after they have been received.

DEFAULT
A failure to make agreed repayments.

DENIAL OF PROBLEMS
Denying a debt problem exists means that it cannot improve and that matters will deteriorate very quickly. Interest accrues on the account and the amount owed will increase all the while. Pretending there is no problem is a way of avoiding the pain of tackling the situation. It takes courage to confront problems face to face, but is an essential first step.

DIRECT DEBIT
A direct debit is an authorisation by a debtor to make regular payments through their bank. The creditor can request amounts that are variable, unlike standing orders where payments are fixed. *see Standing Order*

DISCONNECTION

If you do not make the required electricity, gas or telephone payments you are liable to be cut off. Contact each organisation immediately if you are having problems paying. Offer reduced payment to avoid disconnection. Be economical, keep future bills low; that way it is easier to catch up with your repayments. If you cannot pay and have made no repayment arrangements, Gas and Electricity officials have a right to enter your home, with a warrant, to disconnect the supply. If you are warned of this contact your Social Services Department or DHSS office to see if they can help in any way.

DISCOUNT

When making essential large purchases look around for the best deal. Many retailers sell at discounted prices. Bear in mind that your commodity may need servicing in the future. Be careful not to sacrifice this after sales care for a very low price deal with no back up – it may prove to be a false economy.

DISTRESS WARRANT

A Distress Warrant gives authority to the Bailiffs to enter your home and seize goods which can then be sold to pay your debts. This is usually a last resort when all other methods to obtain payment have failed. It will not happen without plenty of warning.

Bailiffs cannot force entry into your house and certain goods are exempt from seizure –

- *Fixtures, roughly described as the sort of items you would leave if you were moving house e.g. baths, built-in wardrobes, windows, doors, certain built-in hobs or stoves, together with beds and bedding, a reasonable amount of furniture and your 'tools of the trade'.*

- *Goods belonging to other people (other than a husband or wife) also goods which are being rented, loaned or on hire purchase or a conditional sale agreement to the debtor.*

DIVORCE AND SEPARATION

As well as being the cause of financial hardship, relationship breakdowns can be the result of it. Existing on limited resources and dealing with debt problems puts a great strain on a relationship. Each may blame the other for the difficulties, or take their frustrations out on the person closest to them.

Remind yourselves that you are both on the same side; it is not a battle or a matter of which person is right or wrong. Solving a debt problem within a relationship **requires concerted joint effort;** discussions, planning, understanding and general cooperation.

Although tempting to blame someone or something for your problems, it will have a destructive effect to use your partner as the scapegoat. Go to a debt counsellor or share your worries with a trusted friend. Look at ways of reducing your problems together and keep a positive view of the future.

DO SOMETHING

Remaining inactive in a debt situation is going to make matters worse. Do something. Once you have made the first move **you will feel better.** Make an appointment with the debt counsellor at your local Citizens Advice Bureau. Contact one of your creditors, have they a helpline that you can ring? Start being positive and each step from then on will be easier.

DUE DATES

Regular payments have a date by which they must be made. This will be written into the agreement or defined on the statement. If payment is not received by that date then the account is in arrears. Creditors will usually take some mild action such as sending out a reminder letter. If you do not respond then the letters will become more demanding, with a charge usually being made for each one, increasing the total owed. Under certain circumstances, creditors are entitled to telephone or make personal visits to collect overdue payments.

Keep a careful watch on due dates, as late payments will be recorded, incurring extra expense, possibly affecting your credit rating. If you forget a due date, **contact your creditor immediately.** A note can then be made on your account to that effect saving any further action.

E

ECONOMISING

It can be daunting to be suddenly faced with the necessity to cut down on spending, especially when you did not feel that you were overspending previously. Try to see the process as a positive one, where you and the family are taking steps to help yourselves in a difficult situation. If you see yourself as 'hard done by', it will seem more difficult. By using your imagination and some smart planning, you can cut down dramatically on your outgoings. **Get the family to cooperate.** Each member should record where their cash is going so that you can identify where money is being wasted.

Keep spending to a minimum and cut down temptations:

• Carry only the amount of money you need – make shopping lists and stick to them – leave credit cards at home.

• Don't buy food out – take packed lunches to work or picnics instead of restaurant meals.

Cut down on household costs by:

• Using a microwave rather than conventional cooker where possible.

• Thaw frozen food before cooking.

• Use small amounts of water when boiling food.

• Shut freezer and fridge doors immediately.

• Machine wash full loads of clothes or dishes and use the coolest settings needed to clean efficiently.

• Insulate the house as well as you can.

• DIY stores sell reasonably priced draught excluder strips for doors and windows – thick curtains work well too.

• Lag the hot water tank and reduce the heat setting

if it is possible to do so.
• Shut doors to keep heat in.
• Switch off lights, television and music systems when not being used.
• Turn off the central heating if everyone is out – have the heating unit checked to make sure it is operating efficiently.
• Take showers instead of baths.
• Save plastic carrier bags and use as bin liners.
• Make a compost heap to provide cheap fertiliser for the garden – pile together kitchen waste, grass cuttings and leaves together with a little soil and leave to rot down.
• Get the children to do jobs like washing the car or cleaning the windows – this will involve them in the family's efforts and get them to take a pride in saving money and energy.
• Be aware of wastefulness.
• When buying anything think about extra costs, eg clothes that can only be dry cleaned will turn out to be much more expensive.
• Buy supermarket own name goods instead of the more expensive advertised brands.
• Cut down on meat – as well as saving money the family will be having a healthier diet.
• Look for bargains and bargain stores – read consumer magazines to check what items are the best value – keep money off coupons and use when you next go out to shop.
• Browse around seconds shops, second-hand clothes stores, charity shops, church bazaars and car boot sales. Some amazing bargains can be found.
Cut down on entertainment costs by:
• Getting together with friends for meals at home –

share the work and expense by each providing one course – take it in turns to visit each others home.

• Rent a video or watch television rather than visiting the cinema or theatre.

• Swop magazines and books with a friend to halve costs.

• Borrow books, audio and video tapes from the library instead of buying.

• Form a baby-sitting circle.

• Set up a car sharing scheme at work with colleagues or with other parents for running the children around.

• Explore nearby towns and museums and art galleries. Go walking or picnicing in nature parks or local beauty spots. Write letters rather than make expensive phone calls.

• Look upon economising as a challenge and get into the habit of reducing costs.

• Practise being sparing with whatever you use – cut down slightly on amounts of cleaning materials used, such as washing up liquid, polish, washing powder and so on. The job will be completed as effectively without being 'heavy handed' with products.

By changing attitudes to become less wasteful and more cost-effective, the pay off will be substantial savings to your budget.

EDUCATION

Learning extra skills is not only enjoyable, it also increases your earning potential. This is no short-term solution to financial difficulties but viewed long-term may lead to the end of your debt problems and a higher standard of living.

Some options are:
Evening classes • Self education – use the library or buy books on a subject that interests you • Open University Degree • Home Study Courses.
For the unemployed:
TOPS courses – Government sponsored training courses open to anyone over sixteen • Vocational courses at colleges – full and part time • Residential courses at education colleges – grants may be available
Your local Citizens Advice Bureau will point you in the right direction and your library contains a vast source of information.

ELECTRICITY

As electricity officials can enter your home, with a warrant, to cut off supplies if you have not paid, it is essential to contact them if you are having problems paying. It is vital to have heating and lighting and the means to cook meals, so **fuel bills are a priority.** Write, telephone or go into the local office. Make an offer of payment that you can realistically maintain. There are many ways in which payment can be made easier. Maybe a 'slot' meter would help so that you could pay as you used the fuel. This would also make it easier to monitor the amounts being used, so that you could economise where possible.

EMBARRASSMENT

If you are embarrassed to be having financial problems it shows you are a conscientious person, otherwise you would not be concerned. **Do not let embarrassment stop you sorting out your problems.** Debt counsellors have seen many cases similar to yours and it is not their job to reproach anybody or make moral judgements. Quite the contrary, they will be sympathetic and do their best to help make the process as painless as possible.

EVENING CLASSES

Evening classes are an enjoyable way to increase your skills. Unemployed and elderly people get reduced rates. The subject range is extensive with something to interest most people. Extra qualifications mean more chances of employment, a better job, promotion or the opportunity to set up your own business. At the very least you will enjoy the company of others, experience the mental stimulation of learning something new and feel better for doing something positive.

EVICTION

see Bailiffs and Shelter

EXPENDITURE

When listing expenditure **include everything** that has to be paid out. This includes some or all of the following *(everyone's list will differ):*

Housing costs • rent/mortgage, water rates, insurance, gas, electricity, other fuels

Housekeeping • food, cleaning materials, clothes, car insurance and running costs, TV rental & licence, entertainment

Credit commitments • car, washing machine, credit cards, loans etc.

F

FALLING BEHIND WITH PAYMENTS

Once in arrears, problems escalate and become out of control very quickly. Many debtors allow this to continue and their debts to mount because they do not know what to do about it. The first thing is to make contact with creditors and/or an independent debt counsellor. As you begin to take steps to sort your problems it becomes apparent how much expertise and assistance is available to make the process easier. **Creditors will welcome an approach** if you are committed to settling your account as quickly as you can and will have measures that can help. They may accept reduced payments for a while, or suspend the interest temporarily to reduce the outstanding amount more quickly. These are at the discretion of the creditor and your willingness to work at settling the debt will influence how much help you are given.

FAMILIES

Many people try to struggle on alone, bearing the burden with the intention of shielding family members from the harsh facts. This tends not to work, as others, including small children will be aware of the tension. It can be **very constructive to share the problems with the immediate family.** Even if the initial reaction is shock. Once the details are clear, the cooperation of others can be enlisted maybe in simple ways like economising, to larger commitments like older children increasing their contribution to household expenses, or getting part-time jobs to pay for their clothes and entertainment.

Partners and children can be more supportive than expected and problem sharing is often a good way of getting the family to work together for its mutual benefit.

FEAR

Fear and embarrassment are the main reasons for preventing people from facing debt problems. To counteract fear, do something positive and refuse to let others' opinions have any influence; being afraid of what they may say to, or about, you will stop you getting the help you need. Your problems will only be prolonged and made a lot worse.
Have the courage to speak to all those involved, so that appropriate steps can be taken to improve your situation. There is not a person alive who has not made a mistake – nobody is perfect. It is said that the best business people are those who have reached rock bottom and learned from their mistakes. If they had been too afraid of what others might say, they would never have achieved eventual success.

FILLING IN FORMS

When filling in forms, make sure that the information is correct – in most cases it is an offence not to do so. Be sure you fully understand every part of any agreement that you sign. It is imperative to read all the terms and conditions very carefully. **Do not be pressured into signing anything** before you are ready. Take your time. If you have doubts, get impartial advice so that you understand the full extent of what you are taking on. The Citizens Advice Bureau can help if you take a copy along to show them.

FINANCE HOUSES

A broad term used to describe a company that extends credit, ie lends money.

FINANCIAL STATEMENT

A financial statement is a complete assessment of your financial situation. It is put together by drawing up a list of money coming into the home *(income)* and list of all the money that is spent *(expenditure or outgoings)* together with a list of oustanding debts. The expenses are deducted from the income and what is left is apportioned between creditors, with priority debts dealt with first. The severity of financial difficulty is determined and a repayment plan worked out.

If you are managing your financial situation without help, it is essential to draw up a financial statement. Creditors will want to know the state of your finances if you are trying to negotiate reduced payments. They will want to see for themselves that you cannot pay more. If you arrange to see a debt counsellor, they will help compile a financial statement; it will help immensely to do as much of the preparatory work as possible before seeing them.

The statement is worked out on either a weekly or monthly basis – usually depending on whether you are paid weekly or monthly. All sources of income are listed: wages, benefits, maintenance payments, contributions from non-dependants and so on. The outgoings list takes into account everything that is spent including mortgage or rent, water rates, fuel, travelling expenses, housekeeping, school meals, clothing, telephone, child-minding, insurance, TV licence/rental etc. All your debt arrears *(where you are behind with payments)* need to be listed, so that you can work out how much money to allocate to each creditor.

FINANCIAL SERVICES

All the credit facilities such as loans, overdrafts, credit cards, leasing, hire purchase etc that a financial company would offer.

FREEPHONE INFORMATION LINES

Telephone helplines which begin with 0800 are a free service to the user. *see also Helplines*

FUN

Cultivate a sense of fun. Life may be hard going at present but it does not help to take everything too seriously. Get out into the fresh air. Go for a walk along the beach or in the countryside. Invite friends round for an inexpensive meal. Play some board games or cards. Choose to watch only light-hearted and funny films and television programmes. Listen to music that you enjoy and is uplifting. By introducing fun and enjoyment into life you will find that you have much more energy to cope with your problems.

G

GAMBLERS ANONYMOUS
see Addictions

GAS
see Electricity

GIVING UP
Don't – there is always a way. Read through the book again; there is a lot of help and support available to see you through this difficult time. Problems do not last forever. If you feel stuck, try to be more positive. Contact someone else who will just listen to your problems *see Samaritans*. You will find that things begin to move again and you feel better. The process might seem a slow one, but providing you stick with your repayment plan and budget, the day will come when your problems are behind you.

GOING IT ALONE
If your financial problems are fairly simple, then the chances are that you can put things right without too many people becoming involved. But if you have already missed payments, you will need to involve others so that they can advise, or negotiate a repayment plan for what you owe.

You need not feel either ashamed or a failure by admitting you have problems, in fact the reverse is true as it takes courage to face your responsibilities.

GUARANTOR
A Guarantor is a person who takes ultimate responsibility in a credit agreement – if you do not keep up

repayments, they are obliged to take over the debt. The creditor may feel that because of some factor such as your age or employment, the risk in allowing you the money is too great. Having another person, able to fulfil the creditor's requirements and who is willing to make the payments should you default, reduces that risk. The guarantor faces the risk of having to make the repayments with the resultant damage to their credit-worthiness if they cannot.

H

HABIT OF BORROWING

If borrowing *(using credit)* has become a habit that causes you difficulty, **revert to paying with cash,** at least until your finances are more secure.
Stop using credit for purchases such as food, clothes and entertainment. This may reduce your outgoings and allow your finances to recover. If it does, then it is probably because you are more watchful about where your money is going. Paying by cash leaves you in no doubt as to how much you are spending and helps you resist temptation.

HEAD IN THE SAND

When finances are getting muddled, it is tempting to pretend that there isn't a problem or that it will sort itself out. All that will happen is that problems will build up.
Creditors will probably be deciding what action to take – reminder letters, phone call etc. If they do not receive any explanation from you, they may conclude that you are trying to get away without paying, as they cannot know whether your problems are temporary or not.
Far better that you contact them before they have to contact you. If the problem is minor and you can resume regular payments shortly, then no further action is likely to be taken; if the problems are going to take longer to resolve, then the sooner communications are established and a repayment plan started, the easier it will be.
If it all seems too daunting, go to a debt counsellor at the Citizens Advice Bureau, who will be able to

advise you on the best course of action and contact creditors on your behalf if necessary.

HELPLINES

As a first step, making a phone call is one of the easiest and most comfortable ways. Many advice agencies and credit companies have financial helplines and the staff manning the phones will be experienced in dealing with debt difficulties.
Check the telephone directory, benefit leaflets and credit account statements for details of special numbers to ring. If the helpline number begins with 0800, you will not be charged for the call.

HIRE PURCHASE

Items bought on hire purchase **do not belong to you until the last payment is made,** unlike a credit sale where you own the goods at once. Repayments are similar, with an initial deposit followed by regular weekly or monthly payments. If you default the goods can be repossessed. The Company does not have to go to Court to take them back, if you have paid less than a third of the total price.

HOBBIES

A hobby is a good way to forget about problems for a while. When financial troubles are a feature in your life, escaping for short periods, will help you to cope and keep things in perspective.

Your hobby might also prove to be a possible source of extra income. Could you sell what you produce, or market your talents or knowledge for the benefit of others? *see LETS Link*

HOMELESSNESS

see also Shelter

If you think you are going to be made homeless, go **immediately** for advice to the Citizens Advice Bureau or Social Security office.

I

INCOME

When making out a financial statement, you need to list all sources of money that you receive.

These include:

- *Wages, including overtime, for yourself and your partner.*
- *Any Social Security benefits that you claim.*
- *Maintenance payments, pensions whether retirement or other.*
- *Any other income, eg from a lodger.*

INCOME SUPPORT

If your income is very low you may be eligible for income support. Enquire at your local Social Security office for help to cover certain housing costs.

INCREASING YOUR MORTGAGE TERM

It may be possible to arrange with your Bank or Building Society an increase in the term of your mortgage *(this is restrictive upon your age, as there is usually a limit over which companies will not lend).* Increasing the time you have to pay your mortgage means that the payments are reduced accordingly, thus easing immediate financial pressure. This option could solve some of your problems, provided prudent budgeting is continued at least until financial stability is regained.

INFLATION

When working out your budget or calculating whether you can afford an item on credit, **remember to take inflation into account.** Even when inflation drops, it means the rate at which prices increase is slowing – but they are still going up, just at a slower rate, so as time goes by we pay more. If wages rise at the same rate, then its effect won't be drastic, but if they do not, you may find yourself over-committed. Try to save an amount of money to cover inflation and unexpected expenses.

INSOLVENCY

see Bankruptcy

INSURANCE

Reputable credit companies will offer credit protection insurance to safeguard you should there be a downturn in your financial situation. **Ask for details** when taking out any credit agreement. Most building societies offer a sickness and redundancy insurance on mortgages. Having this protection will take away the anxiety and pressure of how you would manage financially should either of these eventualities occur. Insurance cover is available for most of the major life happenings that can wreak financial havoc. **Seek the help of an independent financial adviser** who is not tied to any particular company. They will be able to select the best policy to suit.

INTEREST RATES

Charging interest, over and above the sum of money being loaned, is how creditors make the money to keep their business going. Base rate is the central rate set by the Bank of England. Creditors then add on their own margin which varies from one to another. Just how much interest is charged can make a huge difference to the total amount paid on a credit agreement. Many financial problems arise from an ignorance of how interest charges work. It is essential that they are calculated accurately before taking on credit.

J

JOB CENTRES

Your local Jobcentre can advise about career changes and training as well as being a major source of information about job vacancies.

JOINT AGREEMENTS

A credit agreement taken out in joint names carries joint and several liability. This means that each partner is responsible for the full amount of the debt. Should one of the parties default, then each person will be pursued until the debt is paid in full. Even if you have an arrangement with your partner and have paid your share, you will still be liable for the full amount if your partner tries to evade payment.

K

KEEP RECORDS

When dealing with any aspect of your finances it is much easier to be able to locate the relevant details easily. **Assemble all the letters, bills, documents and agreements** that you hold.

Organise a simple filing system with a box file or a cardboard box with alphabetical card dividers. File your paperwork away, keeping the box safe but accessible. List your payments and the dates due. Check to ensure that you do not miss or are late making payments, as this will incur extra cost for you *(most companies charge for reminder letters)* and will affect your credit rating *(whether or not you are considered a good credit risk in the future)*. Set up direct debits or standing orders at your bank, the payments are made automatically. Make copies of the letters you send and clip them to the corresponding agreement, bill, letter, demand etc. Make notes of when telephone calls were made and what was said. Record dates and amounts of payments sent, so that you have it to hand for future reference.

If it becomes necessary to work with a debt counsellor, it will make the task easier and quicker if you have the facts and figures all together in an ordered system.

KEEP HEALTHY

It is essential to actively take care of your health – especially in times of stress. Even if money is short **try to eat healthily.** Centre your diet on fresh fruit and vegetables with cereals, bread, pasta and rice as the bulk. **Take regular exercise.** A walk costs nothing and does wonders for both looks and level of fitness. Find a sport and participate at least once a week. **Learn the art of relaxation.** To be able to relax at will can be the greatest antidote to worry, anxiety and pressure. Whenever you feel yourself getting anxious about your problems, stop what you are doing, take five deep, slow breaths and resume activity when you feel calmer, *see Relax.* Keep a healthy mental attitude by being positive in whatever you say and do.

KNOW YOUR LIMITS

Financially

Be realistic about what you can afford. Keep strict tabs on exactly what is coming in and going out, **do not overspend.** It is harder to 'fool' yourself and easier to avoid temptation if you are fully aware of the facts.

Mentally

Try not to put too much pressure on yourself. Do your best to find the right solutions but do not blame yourself for the situation. **Cultivate a relaxed attitude** to give you more energy and release constructive ideas to improve your situation.

Physically

Strike a balance between activity and rest. Working hard to overcome problems is fine, but do not push yourself to the point of exhaustion. Throwing oneself into a whirl of activity is often a way of forgetting troubles *(a workaholic).* Take regular breaks and get plenty of sleep to avoid falling prey to illness.

L

LEGAL AID

Find out if you qualify for legal aid to help you sort out your debt problems, especially if your creditors are resorting to extreme measures to recover their money. Your financial situation would need to be assessed to see if you were eligible for the scheme. If so, you would be able to get advice from a solicitor or be represented in a Court case. The Citizens Advice Bureau have a list of solicitors who handle legal aid cases.

LETS LINK

LETS or Local Exchange Trading System is a multi-choice bartering system, enabling local people to give and receive services from one another, without the need to spend money. It puts you in touch with a variety of local resources and all kinds of skills, while helping you stretch a tight budget. The scheme is a non-profit service organised by local people, with groups all around the country.
Members exchange their skills for credits which they can then redeem for goods and services supplied by others in the group. The skills, goods and resources on offer depend on the number of people in each group, but the range can cover everything from accountancy, bricklaying and foreign language lessons to gardening, window cleaning and looking after pets. The LETSystem is an excellent way of enhancing your way of life while getting the satisfaction of being able to do the same for others. All it costs is your time and effort. LETSLink co-ordinate all the various schemes in the UK and can also

provide information on how to start up your own system.

Contact:

Liz Shepherd • LETSLink
61 Woodcock Road • Warminster
Wilts BA12 9DH *Telephone 0985 217871*

LIBRARIES

Libraries are a wonderful free source of information and ideas. Large town libraries contain a far greater range; smaller ones will always try to obtain requested books. It will provide reading which caters to most tastes, a way of filling some time enjoyably and forgetting your problems for a while. The reference section will supply you with specialised knowledge on almost any subject. The atmosphere is always calming and soothing – somewhere to browse in peace and quiet – a retreat from the hustle and bustle.

LOAN SHARKS

see also Money Lenders

Do not fall prey to people who offer to lend money *'no questions asked'*. They will let you have whatever you want but **the cost is enormous.** Repayment charges are set high to begin with and when you are unable to repay, these illegal money lenders resort to unpleasant tactics to retrieve their money. You or your family may be threatened or the lender will try to take your benefit book. They may try to persuade you to take out further loans to clear your debt and so on until matters are out of control. **Never become involved in extra borrowing** when you have debt problems. Seek expert help and guidance first and foremost.

M

MAIL ORDER CATALOGUES

Many mail order companies give a period of interest free credit, only charging interest on more expensive items with payment spread over a longer period. Most companies charge **full retail price** though, so before buying, **compare with items on sale at other outlets.**

MANAGEABLE COMMITMENT

The ideal is when you can comfortably afford all your monthly repayments together with life's essentials and some luxuries. If you are having financial problems and are working to discharge your debts and stabilise your finances, this is the goal to aim for.

MANAGING MONEY

Managing money is a skill learnt throughout life. Some people learn the value of money as well as it's potential pitfalls early on. *see Children* For others, using money sensibly may be learnt later after a few hard lessons. Money is neither good nor bad, it is simply a resource in our society. We have the choice, of if and when we spend, also where and how much. **Choosing wisely** is the key to good money management.

Ask yourself the following when buying anything, especially non-essentials:

- *Do I really need this item?*
- *Can I afford it?*
- *Am I getting value for money?*
- *How will buying this affect my financial stability?*

Undervaluing ourselves is a way of mismanaging money. Most of us could expand and develop the skills and abilities we possess to make life more profitable and fulfilling.

MATERNITY LEAVE

Planning a family needs to include financial forward planning. The resulting drop in income when a parent gives up work, either temporarily or permanently, is the cause of many debt problems. **Reduce commitments to a minimum** and within the budget of the remaining income **well in advance,** to avoid getting into financial *'deep water'*.

MAXIMISE YOUR INCOME

There are many things that you could do to bring in extra income, making extra money available to clear debts and giving you added quality of life. Is there any possibility of a pay-rise at work? Would it not be worth summoning up the courage to ask? The worst that could happen is that the answer comes back as 'No'. Is there a possibility of applying for a better paid position with your present employers or elsewhere? Could you or one of the family work part-time?

Have you checked if your tax code is correct recently, and whether you are getting your full allowances? Are you claiming all the state benefits to which you are entitled? Maybe your hobbies or spare time activities could be used to make a financial profit for you.

see LETSLink

MEND AND MAKE DO

Can you revamp any of your clothes, your home and possessions, to save buying new until your finances recover? Check your wardrobe to see if alterations or mending would extend the life of your clothes. See if it is possible to mend broken household goods, before throwing away. Boxes, plastic containers and glass jars can be reused for storing items in the kitchen or workshop. **Prolong the use of whatever you have available** and it will save money. *see Economising*

MONEY LENDERS

The majority of banks and reputable credit companies, are licensed and strictly controlled by consumer protection laws. But there are less reputable companies that offer to lend that do not respect such restrictions. They operate a 'no questions asked' system charging exorbitant interest, giving the debtor little chance of completely repaying the debt. Their methods of recovering the money range from harassment to violence and blackmail. *see Loan Sharks*
If you are involved with this type of creditor contact your trading standards officer, the Citizens Advice Bureau or the Police.

MONEY ADVICE CENTRES

Money Advice Centres specialise in debt problems and offer free information and assistance. These centres tend to be in large towns and cities. Check the telephone directory to see if there is one near you.

N

NATIONAL DEBTLINE

National Debtline is a telephone helpline offering confidential, expert advice – the number is **021-359-8501.**

Every caller is sent a free information pack giving advice on how to work out a personal budget, how to deal with priority debts, how to make reasonable offers of payment to creditors and how to cope with court procedures.

The phones are manned on Monday and Thursday from 10am to 4pm and on Tuesday and Wednesday from 2pm to 7pm.

NO

Are you easily swayed by salesmen and find it hard to say *No*? When you arrive home with a new purchase or credit agreement, do you ever regret your decision, especially if you have over-committed yourself?

If you are the kind of person who feels uncomfortable saying *No* then remember that being a 'pleaser' can be expensive! **Practice being assertive** so that you have control over your life and finances.

Make a habit of **knowing the state of your finances** – always fill in cheque book stubs and adjust balances accordingly. You can assess quickly whether or not you can afford an item. If you can't, truthfully say to the salesperson 'I can't afford it'. Most sales people will let the matter go, there is no point in trying to sell to someone who hasn't got the money. If you do not want an item, a firm but polite refusal is all that is needed.

NON-PRIORITY DEBTS

Some creditors have authority to take severe action when recovering their money. *see Priority debts* Others do not, regardless of how much pressure they put on you. Non-priority debts are: credit card, unsecured loans and hire purchase agreements. A debt counsellor can advise you on the best way to allocate your money to repay what you owe.

O

OFFERS OF PAYMENT

Making an offer of payment to your creditor will usually stop or delay further action being taken against you. Although not ideal, a creditor will welcome a payment in preference to no payment at all. **Explain your circumstances** – how much is coming in and what your debts are – then offer to pay as much as you can. The creditor will require regular updates so that if your situation improves you can increase the payments, to clear the debt as soon as possible.

OPEN UNIVERSITY

To qualify for one of more than 250 available courses you need to be eighteen or over. You can work towards a degree, diploma or certificate. The qualifications gained are equal to any other university, and recognised by employers and professional bodies. Study materials are sent to your home and the courses involve making use of television and radio programmes, video and audio cassettes or other study aids. Study Centres are spread throughout the UK where you will meet other students at regular tutorials and in informal groups. Tutors and counsellors are available to guide you through your studies and some can be reached by telephone if you need help. Most fees are payable by instalment. If you're unemployed or on a low income you may qualify for financial help.

For details write to:

Central Enquiry Service • The Open University
P O Box 200 • Milton Keynes MK7 6YZ

ORGANISE

It is not easy to get an accurate picture of your finances when things are in a muddle. Try to sort your papers into an ordered system. *see Keep Records* Make sure you know when payments are due and that they are made in time – set up standing orders so they are paid automatically. Late payments often incur charges and these extras may mean the difference between being 'in the red' or 'in the black'.

OUTGOINGS

see Expenditure

OVER-COMMITMENT

When taking credit, remember **there is a limit to which you can go** whilst comfortably making the necessary repayments and having enough money over to cover essentials. Most credit firms do their best to ensure that they only lend to those who can afford to pay, but ultimate responsibility is the borrower's. Over-stretching your financial budget will lead to personal hardship and the risk of losing any future borrowing facility.

OVERDRAFTS

A bank overdraft is an agreed borrowing facility, not an automatic right for account holders. The charges added to your account for going overdrawn are dramatically **higher for unarranged borrowing** and the risk of cheques being returned unpaid, with resultant charges, can be a cause of personal and financial embarrassment. If you need an overdraft facility **contact your bank** to discuss arranging one in advance.

P

PERSONAL LOANS

Personal loans carry a fixed rate of interest with fixed repayments, an advantage when staying within a budget. As with any borrowing, make sure that you can comfortably afford the repayments before committing yourself.

PLAN YOUR FUTURE

Forward planning will ensure a positive outcome. The amount of a person's money is not as important as how well they organise what they do have and how positive their attitudes are. Mental preparation is as important as practical planning. *see Budgeting*
It does matter how you view yourself and your future. Decide what you want for yourself, then **hold that image as your goal.** Don't waver from it. Convince yourself that your prospects are grim, and things will turn out that way – refuse to look on the dark side and the outcome will reflect your thoughts. Concentrate on the good things in life – the things that you have, rather than those that you have not. Stick within your budget, then relax knowing that you are doing your best.

POSSESSION ORDER

If a Court grants a Possession Order on your property, you will have to leave by the date set and the property will be sold to pay off the mortgage. Should the sale not raise enough to clear the full amount owing, then you are still liable for the balance. It is possible that the Bank or Building Society will sell the house quickly at a price lower than market value

to recoup their money, which means that you could lose a substantial amount.
Avoid getting into this desperate situation by contacting your mortgage lender as soon as financial problems are imminent *see Repossession.*

PRIORITY DEBTS

These debts need to be paid first to ensure that you keep a roof over your head, avoid repossession, bankruptcy and imprisonment. Some creditors take drastic action to recover their money so it is necessary to **sort out which is which** and any available money goes to pay the important ones first.
Do not immediately respond to the creditor who 'shouts loudest' or threatens the most, as they might not be the one who can do the most damage. A debt counsellor will be able to sort out which of your debts are priority and non-priority and advise you accordingly.

PROTECTION SCHEMES

see Insurance

R

RAINY DAY FUND

Debt counsellors will recommend you **save some of your income,** however tight your budget. There will always be unexpected expenses arising, such as emergency repairs. Without taking account of this your budget will be unworkable. If you suddenly have to use money allocated to creditors, it may mean you are back to square one. Having a rainy day fund will provide the means to deal with emergencies and remove some of the anxiety about coping.

REDUNDANCY

Being made redundant can have devastating psychological and financial effects. Try not to feel overwhelmed – **tackle the practical issues right away.** If you were employed full-time then you are almost certainly entitled to compensation. **Write immediately to your ex-employers** to claim, appeal to an Industrial Tribunal if they do not pay out within a few months. You may also be able to get legal aid if necessary.

In the case of your Company going into liquidation, you should receive redundancy payments – make a claim to the Department of Employment who are responsible for them.

Contact your creditors to explain your circumstances and seek specialised advice to help work out a plan to handle your finances.

Meanwhile, **do everything you can to get another job.** This will keep you occupied and motivated. Redundancy brings feelings of hopelessness and despair – do not let these feelings drag you down.

However many job applications you send off you only need one job, so never give up. A positive attitude will bring a positive result.

RELAX

Tension can drain your energy and reduce your ability to handle problems. To counteract worry, find time to relax. Getting sufficient sleep is a great help, but learning how to relax while awake is an excellent way to calm the mind and rest it from the stresses and strains of financial worry.

The benefits of relaxation are calmer and clearer thinking when under pressure, improved physical health and well-being, and an increased sense of optimism.

There are techniques you can learn that will help you more each time you practice them

5 Deep Breaths

A simple way to relax is to stop whatever you are doing when you feel uptight and take five slow, deep breaths. Breathe in through your nose and out through your mouth. Concentrate on your breathing – try to still your mind and stop the flow of thought. Imagine all your muscles relaxing and mentally and physically just let go. Resume normal activity but approach everything calmly.

10 Minute Break

Take a relaxing 10 minute break at some time during the day. Find a quiet place to lie down and put your feet up, preferably so that they are slightly higher than your head. Concentrate on your breathing, keeping it slow and steady. Bring to mind some pleasant scene, such as a lovely garden or peaceful beach and spend the next few minutes right there in your mind. Soak up the sunshine, the beauty and the peace of that place. Enjoy the good feelings as though you were really there. If you find other thoughts intruding, gently push them away and return to your centre of calm. Take a minute or so to come back. Stretch and get up slowly, gently returning to your surroundings.

When going to sleep and waking

To stop the flow of worrisome thoughts at night, practice drifting off peacefully. Take slow controlled breaths and concentrate on positive and happy thoughts. Whatever is on your mind as you go to sleep generally determines the kind of nights sleep you get – troubled thoughts = restless sleep, happy thoughts = peaceful sleep. Repeat the process for a couple of minutes on awakening to put you in a positive frame of mind to face the day.

RELAXED ATTITUDE

Always try to retain a relaxed attitude. This doesn't mean an uncaring and irresponsible attitude, rather a sense of proportion on events and circumstances. Don't over dramatise and make out that things are worse than they are. Do your best, but do not work yourself into a frenzy of activity or worry. Take time for yourself and cultivate an appreciation of the simple things in life – a walk in the country or on the beach can restore a sense of stability and equilibrium, giving fresh insight and a new surge of energy.

RENT ARREARS

If you fall into arrears with your rent, you run the risk of being evicted. Whether you live in council or private property it is important to tell your landlord that you are having problems. Rent or mortgage arrears are **priority debts and must be dealt with first.** Private landlords tend to be less sympathetic than councils, as they probably depend on your rent as income. Nevertheless avoiding the issue is likely to increase the landlords anger and hasten an eviction order. Explain the circumstances to the rent collector and do your utmost to work out a way of making regular payments and clearing the arrears. Meanwhile it may be worth looking around for cheaper accommodation. Remember though that you would still be liable for the debt after you have moved.

If you are a council tenant making regular payments and at least some effort to clear your arrears, it is unlikely that you will be evicted. If your home is too large or too expensive to heat, discuss moving to a more economical council property.

If you have received a notice to quit, seek immediate advice from the Citizens Advice Bureau – you may be eligible for legal aid. If you receive a Court Summons you must attend the hearing. Your solicitor will explain your financial circumstances and if you make a reasonable offer of payment it is unlikely the Judge will order eviction.

REPOSSESSION

Whoever holds your mortgage – Bank or Building Society – will only repossess your home as a last resort. To avoid this happening, go to the **lending manager and explain your problems** as early as possible. Mortgage arrears, like rent arrears are priority debts and you need to do your best to pay these before any others to keep the roof over your head.

Never consider handing back the keys to your home *(voluntary repossession)*. You will have nowhere to live, or have to find money to rent somewhere. Your house debt will also be increasing as interest accrues to the outstanding loan. When the house is sold you will be charged the sale costs *(agents, lawyers, etc)*. If there is negative equity in the property *(where the property is worth less than the debt)* the mortgage company will pursue the customer until the debt is cleared. Most importantly, you will not be able to claim any housing benefit or have the chance of a council property, as you will have *intentionally* made yourself homeless.

S

SAMARITANS

The Samaritans are a voluntary organisation open 24 hours a day, every day of the year. They listen to and support those in despair. You can ring the number in the phone book anytime, or call into their office, no appointment is needed. You can rely on complete confidentiality.

Talking out feelings and discussing problems is so very necessary – holding everything in can make matters seem much worse. The Samaritans provide a befriending and listening service to those who need it. They have helped thousands in times of crisis.

SECOND MORTGAGE

Taking out a second mortgage *(remortgage)* releases equity on your home and is a way to raise capital to pay off debts. Your mortgage payments will increase, but the interest charges are low. The term may be different, probably shorter than the original. You do of course risk your home should you default.

SECURED LOAN

This is a loan where you are asked to provide additional security, such as your house, shares or life insurance policy. These are pledged as a guarantee and you risk losing them if you cannot keep up the repayments.

SEEKING HELP

The message repeated over and over in this book, has been **seek help**. There are people well

qualified to give advice and assistance who offer their expertise, in many cases without charge.
Take advantage of all the help and support available. Although people with financial problems often feel ashamed or embarrassed don't let it prevent you from seeking help. Remember, you are not alone in your predicament – many people are experiencing severe financial difficulties and it is a common problem; so much so that creditors now have people on their staff to deal specifically with accounts that have run into difficulty.
The first step is the most difficult to take, but after that, when you see that there are workable solutions and people sympathetic and eager to help, the process becomes easier and the future brighter. *see Helplines and Citizens Advice Bureaux*

SELF-EMPLOYED

The self-employed face a somewhat different situation when facing financial difficulty. They cannot claim unemployment benefit, although they are entitled to other benefits – check the Social Security office or Citizens Advice Bureau. An accountant should be able to advise whether you are claiming the business expenses to which you are entitled.
Being self-employed often carries with it, feelings of making it on your own – try not to let pride or embarrassment hold you back from getting the help and support you need.

SHAME

Most people in financial trouble experience feelings of shame and failure, thinking that the situation is their fault and that they will be judged for the way things have turned out. This is the main reason why people are reluctant to ask for help or contact their creditors.

In fact, creditors only want to find a practical and workable way to recover their money. They allow for customers in difficulty, either by way of a telephone helpline, or training staff to use debt counselling skills with customers. Independent debt counsellors will show understanding and sympathy and do their best to protect your interests. The most important point to remember is that it is in the interests of both parties to sort out problems as soon as possible.

Do not allow feelings of shame to prolong a stressful situation – make the first move and those upsetting feelings will decrease. Your self-esteem will return as you take responsibility for dealing with your situation.

SHELTER

If you have a housing problem and don't know what to do, if you are being threatened with eviction, if your home is no longer safe or you are being harassed or if you are homeless you can contact *Shelter*, a registered charity with 28 centres located throughout England, Scotland and Wales. They offer advice to people who are homeless, potentially homeless or have housing problems.

Advisers will assist those in immediate need and help them to find temporary accommodation.

In London, *Shelter* provide a free emergency helpline; open all year, weekdays from 6pm to 9am, round the clock at weekends & Christmas.

telephone 0800 446 441

To find your nearest *Shelter* office look in the telephone directory or contact –
Shelter • 88 Old Street • London EC1V 9HU
telephone 071 253 0202

SHOP AROUND FOR GOOD DEALS

When making any purchase it pays to **shop around** – check whether you can buy the same elsewhere for less. If you are using credit, work out the total price, as what might appear cheaper in one shop may turn out to be more expensive with the charges added. Goods that require a maintenance agreement may be offered cheaply if the maintenance is not included, but you may find it costlier long term to pay for servicing and repairs.

SHORT TERM LOANS

If a loan is only required for a short term, you may find that the rates on an overdraft facility could be preferential. **Ask at your bank.**

SIGNING AN AGREEMENT

Ensure that you **always read every word** of an agreement before signing. Get advice if there is anything you do not fully understand. Give yourself thinking time to decide if the purchase is right for you.
see Managing Money – ask yourself the four questions and work out how the repayments will affect your budget

SMALL CLAIMS COURT

If you are owed money and that is contributing to your financial problems, then it may be worth finding out if you could apply for help to the small claims court to recover the debt.

SOCIAL FUND

This is a borrowing facility from Social Security for those receiving benefit. The loans are mainly for 'crisis' purposes and given at the discretion of the individual benefit office. Loans have to be repaid within eighteen months; repayments are deducted directly from the claimant's benefits.

SOCIAL SECURITY

Enquire at your local office, details in the telephone directory, about the benefits to which you might be entitled. *see Benefits*

SOLICITORS

Employing a solicitor *(asuming they will take the case on)* when there is a shortage of money, may well add to the problem. You may be entitled to the services of a Solicitor under the free Legal Aid scheme.
The Citizens Advice Bureau can supply a list of participating solicitors, and are also able to give free advice on debt problems themselves.

STANDING ORDERS

A standing order payment is an amount specified by you and paid direct from your bank account to your creditor. It differs from a direct debit in that the amount paid doesn't vary *see Direct Debit*. Using standing orders to pay for services like gas, electricity, water and council tax can help you budget. You know exactly how much will be paid each month. It saves the bother of having to remember to make a payment and it is possible to pay by standing order for most things bought on credit. As it helps to spread the cost evenly throughout the year, it helps to cushion the shock of receiving large bills.

STORECARDS

Storecards are similar to credit cards but can only be used in a particular store or group. Like credit cards, they are a convenient way to pay, but if you are unable to pay off the total owed each month, they are **an expensive form of credit**, as interest charges tend to be high.

T

TAKE ONE DAY AT A TIME

A human being's ability to look back to the past and into the future has enabled mankind to make great progress. But it is also an ability that gives us the capacity to worry.

First you must **think and act positively** about your problems, and then also cultivate the capacity to take one day at a time. Never agonise over what has happened or live in fear of the future. Reacting negatively simply will not improve matters. You will only feel drained and below par, unable to cope. Focus on **what needs to be done today** and persevere with that.

Take some time for yourself each day. Relax, listen to music and take some exercise. Concentrate on the good things in your life – look around for them if they are not immediately obvious! Whenever you start to fret, remember to focus your mind on something pleasant and positive.

TALENTS

see LETS Link

TALK

see also Advice and Ask

Talking to the right people at the right time can help you handle your finances sensibly. Always **seek expert advice** and ask about any points which are not crystal clear. It is also very important to discuss your worries with someone who will listen and who cares about you. They may not be experienced in understanding debt problems or giving advice, in fact it works much better if they just listen and allow you to let off steam. By expressing your worries, you will relieve stress and feel much better. Having a heart-to-heart with a friend or partner will reduce your burden and leave you feeling lighter and able to cope. Get into the habit of expressing feelings and sharing your thoughts as bottling things up will make matters worse.

TAX

If you pay tax, **make sure the tax office knows of any change in your circumstances.** This may mean an alteration to your allowances. As allowances form part of your income, if less is deducted from your wage you will have extra money available. If your income falls suddenly, then you may be eligible for a rebate.
Tax officers need to be made aware of other changes such as the loss of a spouse, the existence of a disabled family member and the number of dependants you have. The tax office have free information fact sheets.

TELEPHONE DIRECTORY

Use your directory to locate sources of help and advice eg Citizens Advice Bureau, Samaritans, Consumer Advice and Trading Standards. As addresses are listed too, you can visit the relevant office if you prefer. A **phone call or visit to someone** most able to give qualified advice, would be the best step you can take to sort out your problems.

TELEPHONE HELPLINES

National Debtline - 021 359 8501

TEMPTATION

Manufacturers are skilled at presenting their products in the best way to encourage sales. This is good business, but for impulse buyers who are tempted to buy goods they don't need, it is a problem. There are measures which will help you avoid unnecessary spending:

- *Do not go food shopping when hungry.*
- *Take a specific amount of cash on shopping expeditions and leave credit cards at home.*
- *Shop with a friend who knows the problem, to dissuade you from buying on impulse.*
- *Only go to shops that you have to buy from. Resist browsing and 'window shopping'.*
- *Give yourself a pat on the back when you return with only what you set out to buy.*
- *Do you know why you spend money unnecessarily? Does it provide an excitement or interest missing from the rest of your life? Could you find a positive (and less expensive) way of getting the enjoyment you need?*

TERMS AND CONDITIONS

All reputable credit companies will give you a copy of an agreement you are considering taking out. From this you can work out the exact amount that you would be repaying. You **must read and understand** the terms and conditions thoroughly before signing, otherwise **ask for an explanation** of any point you are uncertain of. If you still have doubts, ask again, or take the agreement to an independent adviser. Remember that you may lose your rights to cancel if you sign on the trader's business premises. A similar situation exists if a deal is arranged by phone, even if you sign the agreement at home.

THEFT

- *Cheque book and credit card fraud is widespread, so make sure that you don't make it easy for thieves. Report losses immediately to the bank or credit company, so that a stop on further use can be placed upon them. Retailers then have a chance of catching the thieves and recovering your possessions.*
- *Consider installing an alarm system to protect your home.*
- *DIY stores sell inexpensive 'beepers' to fit windows and doors.*
- *Ask your police station if they operate a security marking service, or if there is a Neighbourhood Watch scheme operating in your area.*
- *Protect your belongings by taking out adequate insurance, see Insurance, although any loss will usually cause you some expense.*

THINK FIRST

One reason for getting into debt is that purchasers do not give enough thought to whether they can afford an item. Give yourself **as much time as possible** before handing over the money or signing an agreement. Work out exactly how the repayment terms will affect your budget. Think whether that purchase is really only an indulgence which will create future problems. Money worries can take the joy out of most things in life. **Ask yourself if it is really worth it.**

If you know you are an impulse buyer, **take only enough money to buy essentials** and leave your credit cards and cheque book at home. Having to make a return journey to the shop might be the deciding factor between what is vital and what is not.

U

UNEMPLOYMENT

Being unemployed can have a very 'depressing' effect; it can alter your outlook on life and reduce your ability to cope. If you have tried unsuccessfully to find work, try to increase your feelings of energy, usefulness and self-motivation. This will put you in a better position, mentally and physically, when a job comes along.

A sense of purpose Channel your energies into something positive. Try decorating the house, helping to start a playgroup or writing a book. You may never have a better chance to be creative.

Activity and routine Keep busy – boredom is stressful. There are always tasks to do. At the end of the day you will have the satisfaction of having cared for yourself and your living space. Develop routines so that each day has a plan.

Identity and self-respect Remember, your identity does not depend on your job. You are not a secretary or a steel worker or whatever your last job was – you are a unique human with potential. Assess your skills and be prepared to try something new. Maybe you have the talents to start a business?

Friendship Keep in touch with friends with whom you can share good and bad times. The company of like-minded people is a tonic that puts problems into perspective, as well as a possible source of information regarding jobs. Keep in touch to make sure you are always first on the scene of potential opportunities.

W

WAIT AWHILE

When considering making a major purchase ensure the decision is right by waiting, at least overnight, before signing any agreement. This will give you the opportunity to take all factors into consideration, and work out carefully whether or not you can afford the item and what the financial consequences will be.

WATER RATES

Contact the water company **as soon as you have a problem** making payments. If you receive Social Security benefit or Income Support, **contact your Social Security office** who can arrange to make regular, reduced payments direct from your benefits.

WILLS

Making a will ensures the people you care for are not left in financial difficulty when you die. It is neither a complicated nor expensive process. Most people assume their estate will go directly to their nearest and dearest, but this is not necessarily so.

Dying intestate *(without having made a will)* means that the law steps in to decide how your assets are shared out. If distant relatives claim, close family can find themselves in financial hardship. If you have no living relatives and die without making a will, everything will go to the government.

Go to a solicitor with the names and addresses of the people to whom you wish to leave property, money or gifts. List everything you own with an

estimate of its worth and subtract from this any money that you owe. The solicitor will give you any necessary advice and draw up the document.
If, after making a will your circumstances alter, it is a simple procedure to change it. The solicitor can make the amendments, which will need to be witnessed in the same way as the original. If you have drawn up your own will, it may be simpler to make out a completely new one.
Keep the will safe, your bank or solicitor should look after it, and make sure that someone close to you knows where to find it.

WINDFALL

If you are lucky enough to come into an unexpected amount of money, then **get expert advice** as to how to get the optimum benefit from it. It makes good sense to clear outstanding debts, as the debit interest you are being charged will be higher than any credit interest you may earn from the sum.

X

XMAS

Christmas can be the worst time of the year if you are working with a tight budget. **Spread the cost** by buying weeks and months beforehand. Decide that you won't be pressured into spending more than you can afford. Family and real friends will understand if you explain that you need to cut back on presents, cards and food. Christmas is only two days in the year and soon forgotten as the New Year arrives and normal routines resume. Is it worth damaging the hard work that has been put in over the past year?

Y

YES

'Yes' – although this is what all sales people want to hear, creditors would prefer you to accept only if you know that you can afford it. The time, cost and losses incurred trying to recover debts are vast and an increasing drain on the credit industry. Taking on a financial commitment you cannot meet will only bring personal misery and hardship.

YOUNG PEOPLE

Most young borrowers *(up to mid thirties)* experience financial problems because they have tended to over-commit themselves, especially with credit cards. For older people the reason is usually changed circumstances.

It is young people who are reluctant to seek advice concerning their finances. Creditors would welcome the opportunity to sort out problems at an early stage with any young customer, as developing good working credit relationships ensures healthy future business.

So whatever your age, **follow the suggestions outlined in this book** – if you have problems, face up to them, seek advice, contact your creditors and start sorting out your financial matters sooner rather than later.

PERSONAL PLAN OF ACTION

- *Complete the following exercises using the forms below. Alternatively use separate sheets of paper if you prefer.*
- *Define your financial problems.*
- *Write down what you think is the cause of your difficulties and the extent they affect you and your family.*
- *Describe your feelings and express your anxieties so that you can look for positive ways of coping .*

List your details either weekly OR monthly

INCOME

Wages .... £

Partner's Wages .... £

Pensions .... £

Social Security Benefits .... £

Maintenance .... £

Contributions from Family .... £

Any Other .... £

TOTAL .... £

EXPENDITURE

Mortgage or Rent .... £
Endowment Policy .... £
Council Tax .... £
Insurances .... £
Water Rates .... £
Gas .... £
Electricity .... £
Coal or other fuel .... £
Housekeeping .... £
School Meals .... £
Fares .... £
Clothes .... £
TV Licence or Rental. .... £
Telephone .... £
Car Costs .... £
Childminding .... £
Court Fines. .... £
Child Maintenance .... £
Any Other .... £
.... £
.... £
TOTAL .... £

PRIORITY DEBTS - Arrears Owing

Mortgage or Rent .... £
Council Tax .... £
Water Rates .... £
Gas .... £
Electricity .... £
Magistrates Court .... £
Child Maintenance .... £
Other .... £
.... £
.... £
.... £
.... £
TOTAL .... £

CREDIT DEBTS - Arrears Owing

Creditors: .... £
.... £
.... £
.... £
.... £
.... £
.... £
.... £
.... £
TOTAL .... £

Deduct expenditure from income and apportion any spare money to creditors. If there is not enough to cover your debts, work out a repayment plan on a pro-rata basis *(read Section 3 in the 10 Point Plan).* A Debt Counsellor can help you with this. Take these sheets and the details of all debts and creditors with you when you go for advice.

List all possible sources of help and advice:

Name *Address* *Phone Number*

Name *Address* *Phone Number*

Name *Address* *Phone Number*

List the Creditors you need to contact – all those to whom you are in arrears:

Name *Address* *Phone Number*

Name *Address* *Phone Number*

Name *Address* *Phone Number*

Write down an explanation of your circumstances, together with details of the steps you are taking to sort out your financial problems and repay your debts.
Refer to this when telephoning or writing to your creditors.

List ways of:
ECONOMISING – cut down on Expenditure

1

2

3

4

5

List ways of:
INCREASING YOUR INCOME

1

2

3

4

5

Who are the people jointly involved in your financial situation and/or affected by the problems?

What do you need to say and to whom?

Write down how you can improve communications with each person, so that everyone is aware of the difficulties and you are all cooperating together to overcome them.

To give yourself objectives to work towards, write down your goals - what do you want to achieve? Make them realistic, but very positive views of how you see yourself and your financial situation in:
3 Months

6 Months

1 Year

5 Years